FYACRACKR

Ruben Whitter

Whittword Publications// Wrighter.

This book is dedicated to those who want to take off and explode in the most resplendent way.

- Ruben Whitter

Drop…

Luster Reshines

In a fiery ballet where molten luster reshines - it gleams
- a painter spills their vibrant hues.
From ember'd citrus to citrine's meandering dreams,
The scrolling light reveals subtle clues...

Brightness spills forth like dawn's first tender kiss,
to excite a marbled index when sunset's blush does spread:
zooming flashes of storied rainbowed bliss
stretched far. A day rings of hums of an echoed tread;

plated with pigment; the sky now oxens anew
as molten strands of bril'yant intertwine-
d volts of starlight drench in vibrant plumes of blue.
A spectrum'd wave in scattered sparks does shine

then, from the core, where preserved emojis blend
a tall tapestry of fertility that unnerves and extends.

A Whisper

As wool galvanises, a whisper turns into
echoes of memories fresh out of their shell,
all from a no cap backup of
a mixture of pictures - both new and old -
held back as: heat that rings a cold spend.
Must this be the way that shows a soul's saving?
Out comes a drop like a star cascading
from heaven, charging the way to the end
of a commotion of emotion that stirred each soul
- each witness - to the dance that appeared because
of shards of devotion that from up high fell
to be caught by their hearts' swollen celestial view.

Heed the crackles - the call for embrace -
and your spirit; will happen to be the one; they will forever chase.

Moonlit Guidance

In moonlit guidance, apple'd diamonds glide
as soft orbs that trail the gentle curve of jest...
Each - a bright spark - where emojis bide
fleeting: blazed hearts grow faint and weak

as if the stars themselves in mourning weep
their journey. Pixel'd in whispers of the night
- in their gleam - the darkest shadows sleep.
Each droplet skates on paths of purest light:

a glittered arc. Across the midnight sky
they burst like fleeting dreams in the gloom,
transforming into a grand sigh:
their brilliance brightens every shadowed room.

In every fruit, a fleeting spark resides,
a beauty born from where the heart confides.

Been Nice

It would have been nice to have a parent
or two; people
like that sort of thing; and
I like the idea of being
considered as
one of the people.

Mad We Pixel

Life's tale: proper mad.
We pixel the prize, me duck…
Twisting: secrets clad.
Moments pass - laugh - then there's luck!
In each turn; we learn and grow.

Heat Wid a Square

Reckon sum 'tween-ear heat?
Wid a square lot o' new tweets
chuck one cross-lot o' honey,
sea salt to yer tummy
'n' lob yer four-sided 'ands… Yeet!

Spark be More

Wonderful! The spark
be more than flicks of the wrist?
In five-seven-five…

Night Path

Tracing di night path;
each gaff a silent story
- dem pain's brief release
rainin' small sparks a ions -
bright'ning the heart's hidden wounds.

Moonlight Night Whispers

Tranquil moonlit night
whispers of stars in motion.
Peaceful dreams take flight;

twilight twinkles bright:
cosmic symphony. Shimm'ring
tranquil moonlit night,

vivid swirls of light:
ethereal eternity echoes
peaceful dreams. Take flight

whispering winds... sigh
royal secrets carried wide!
Tranquil moonlit night-

mountains kiss di sky...
hushed - humbled - trapped in time.
Peaceful dreams take flight

jolted and sparked
by retribution in kind:
tranquil. Moonlit night
peaceful dreams take flight.

Gawpin' Skyward

In flares of brilliance, we converge,
gawpin' skyward as the clouds weep
an exuberant display… a luminescent purge:
each shared second a sworded story for all

gawpin' skyward-as. The clouds' weep
eyes alight with wonder 'n sync:
each shared second a sworded story. For all
in shadows of joy; we dare not to blink

- eyes alight with wonder! In sync;
a symphony of who's in crowds of di light;
in shadows of joy… "We dare not to blink
before this ephemeral dance of angelic delight

- a symphony!" Of who's in crowds of di light;
embracing the scotches of ephemeral crescendos
before this ephemeral dance of angelic delight;
we find unity in this luminous bravado.

Embracing the scotches of ephemeral crescendos
- a jubilant ode to life - but an embrace
we find unity in! This luminous bravado;
in the swirl of dreams; each effervescent phase

a jubilant ode. To life, but an embrace
of exuberant displays, is a communal urge…
in flares of brilliance! We converge;
gawpin' skyward; as the clouds' weep.

FYACRACKR

Yu see dem? Dem deh; seen as dis reyt jammy sod weh cross all local scenes; dem possess a propah knack fih captivate, dem just comman' attention wid dem stunnin' vibes a dem powerful conduits fi express emotions pon global. Dem storied looks-a fya, drippin' wi colour reyt vibran'leh - mek folk gwaan'n gormless awe - etching dem next level moments inna core a all.

Inna coun'less kind a situation, dem deh like inna emotional journey forgin' connections among people and highlightin' the beauty of experiences di fleet, evoking epic powerful feelin's like wundah. Propah strikin', dem straight-up create rad feelings fi di whole community weh stay long after dem dip, but dem still impactful presence.

Dem reyt unexpected sight leave impressions that last, mek memories weh resonate: Craftin' mem'ries that endure 'n' stay deep inna di'art wi' who witness dem; celebrating di essence of shared human experiences and di insane beauty a di transient.

Trees Are Made Fi Burn?

Share - would yuh - in di forest, or di grove?
Some trees ne'er bear fruit. Some trees stay bare
fi di owls fi toot 'bout how much love dem have fi hare
dat flute in di roots inna di dem sanctuary - dem cove....

But some trees just good fi di stove;
fi lik one wi' warmth; as each leaf in di air
is not a page of di heart-would-be-earned-where
but seed fi which way yuh sole should rove.

A drop from above might turn plants lush,
dem might revive emeralds fi motion unshorn,
but be careful where di deluge might fall

as some plants get plant'd and not in a rush
fi grow; other than spikes, other than thorns:
Some grow-a tall, and some nah grow at all.

Glow While Dem Bloom

Dem glow while dem bloom…
embers in di darkened sky:
life's raw explosions.

Shattered illusions – dem broad
like drops a fiery deluge.

Resilience:
upload strength from di marsh.
Not in han', it is

still fi clear a long eat;
an' emerge from di stormy,

veiled, hidden stage.
Courage dance in di flames:
a bril'yant display.

Facets foil 'n' shine new
as di soul dem get it dew.

Duckeh

Duckeh's blackened tread. He dared to rise...
to burst the clouds with audacious graft -
defying di mardy who 'loved'. His cobbed size -

ah kid, his ambition, rainbowed the skies!
His royal scran a feast for his laugh:
Duckeh's blackened! T'read; he dared to rise

past; the barmy - who tried to tie his life,
who would giggle as they twitchell'd his sparkled raft.
Defying di mardy who loved his cobbed size,

he sings "ayup" to those in gravity he finds
shadowed by vibrant dollops of colour - balletically craft,
duckehs! Black 'n' 'read, he dared to rise

through the bubble and squeak of dem sus unmashed hides.
"Gerron with the pettiness that sought to sway 'imself daft
-defying!" Di mardy, who loved his cobbed size...

oh, how he scrolled against with grace untied:
a beacon of dreams! "Giz us an embrace as
Duckeh's blacken'd tread!" He dared to rise;
defying di mardy... who loved his cobbed size.

Summer's Night

In summer's night, the sharin-a light
- exhales of hail - bids di dark to dance
wi' fuse-alight; it begets di light
'n' grants the sky a brief multicoloured trance.

Within di buildup - sparks - dem may fly
where substance awaits the touch of pain;
to burst 'n brilliance - bright against di sky -
'n' fill the air wi' leers as loud as shame.

Yet, heed the drench that turns to roar of might…
for in its fervour, danger may reside:
a fleeting thrill that lights the endless night!
But, caution must attend di festal tide.

Though all di gleam can lift our hearts on high;
in careful hands; its wonder won't deny.

Ballooning Spark

As di leaves dem, drop a stray orb flew
a ballooning spark - a dance of sound and light;
a flick an' a twist: a tale weh ever true.

Cross di blushing sky, its colours dem grew
a burst of citrine in darkness all around
as di leaves dem drop... a stray orb flew.

Wid cracklin' laughter - pickney - dem eyes imbue
di starry canvas stories a trailed flight:
a flick an' a twist, a tale weh ever true.

A fleetin' comet leavin' trails askew...
paints a memory pon hearts spellbound
as di leaves dem drop. A stray orb flew.

Its quick brilliance: a rendezvous!
A wild crescendo would spark great height!
A flick an' a twist - a tale weh ever true.

An' as it would wade the night resumes its cue,
yet whispers linger in di night dem surround
as di leaves dem drop - a stray orb flew...
A flick an' a twist: a tale weh ever true.

Silent Orb

Silent orb released -
unfurling in whispered flight:
hearts meet? In hashes,

stars hide behind morn:
cold echos. "Grip di dark cloud,
night!" Chill dims the sky.

"Fragile." Moments fly,
illuminating the shroud:
touch fades with the dawn.

"Dem nackered." Ashes
softly fall - in muted light -
love's shadow: recede...

Beneath your soft glow; dreams gently unfurl
secrets… in dem, silver swirl.

Restless Soul

Bruv, in shadows where dreams parade,
mi wander through life's arcade...
Frustration's grip tight
mi soul inna di night
- in limbo - where choices dem fade.

Each step mi take mi stumble and sway,
echoes of dreams start fi decay
in flashes: so peak
- mi spirit nuh sleep
but wander - like lost inna play.

A restless soul in di charade
of choices made late like a sage,
Few ambitions dem wilt
but mi spirit a-gilt
from figures that bring dreams to shame.

Hope nuh dead, tide still a-plant
fi rise like di phoenix: avaunt!
Inna embrace so dark,
mi soul find a spark
to conquer dis weary haunt.

Frustration be ova? Mi heart,
mi spirit, ready fi start...
'low it you neek!
Mi soul dem nah keep,
a pris'ner no more..! Mi part

that calls mi stand tall;
mi dreams; rise like waves inna squall!
Frustration nuh win
- mi soul start fi sing
in shadows; mi rise; conquering all.

Silent Balloons

Crystals ignite di sky wid cheer?
Bombasity bring life to di dark air;
crystals ignite di sky wid cheer;
but - lattice pon lattice - dance from di sleigh
in silent balloons. No soft tune:
laterally in di midnight they glare...
Crystals ignite di sky wid cheer!

Grief Echoes

Grief echoes softly through the room
- in shadows - cast by sum cruel jest;
a parent's pride consumes the bloom
of sorrow's right to heartfelt rest.

In shadows cast by sum cruel jest,
pairs mingle wi' the mirror's gaze
of sorrows. Right to heartfelt rest,
but lost in self, they nivver praise

pears. "Mingle wi' di mirror's gaze…"
Reflection's cold. They nick the light,
but lost in self, they nivver praise
the mourning child: left to the night.

Reflections cold, they nick the light
- a parent's pride consumes. The bloom;
the mourning child; left to the night:
grief echoes softly through the room.

Di Wind

Di wind's quiet tune,
driftin' in di moonlight soft...
time a whispah sweet.

British-born poet Ruben Whitter's happenstantial ancestry from Jamaica and beyond contains a rich tapestry of events that he continues to be freshly inspired by: allowing them to gently shape his literary lens as he continues to champion stories of hope; love; and victory through his resplendent pen which is often shaped by his affinity for the chemical sciences. Whitter's gen-z societal experiences, through his upbringing in Nottingham, can also be seen fragranced within his works.

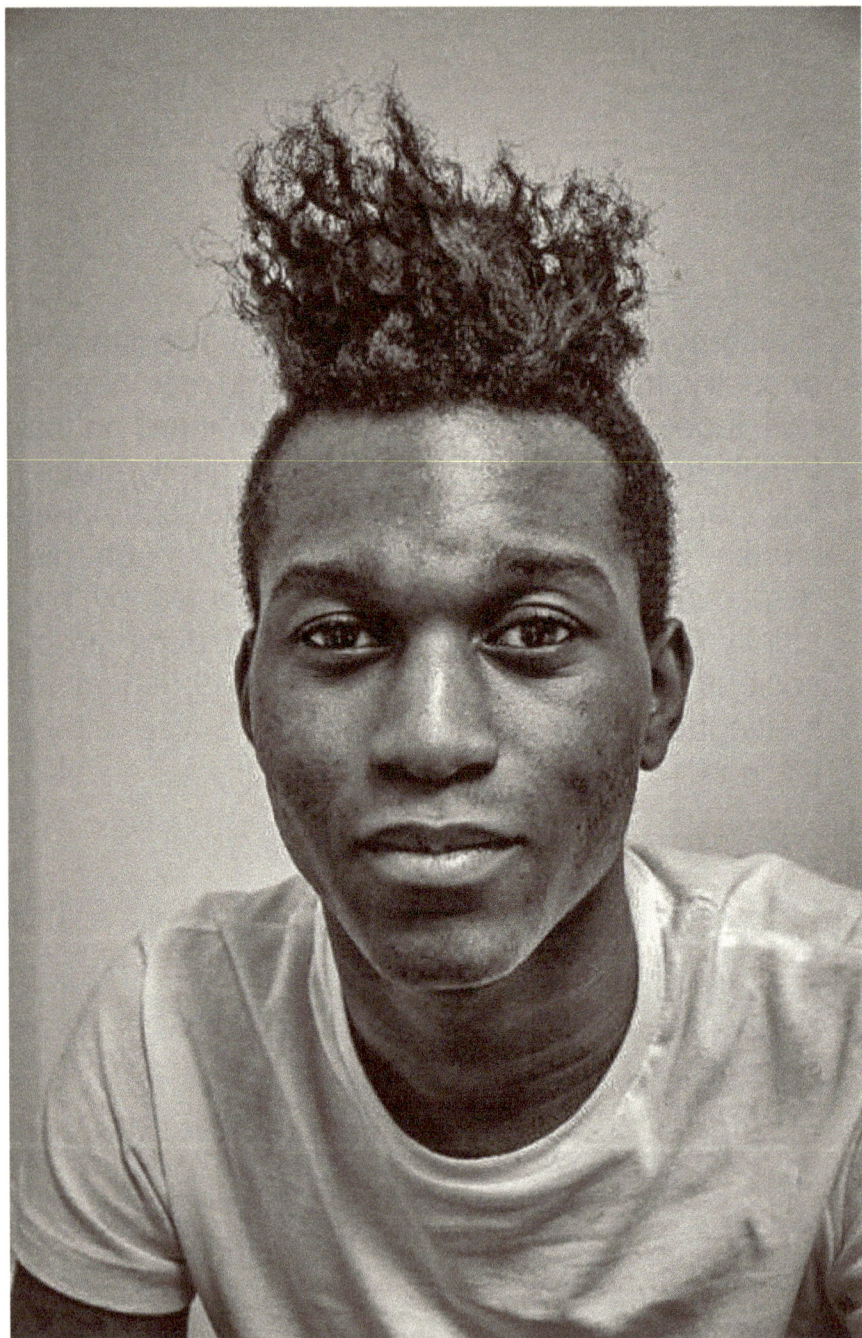

www.ingramcontent.com/pod-product-compliance
Lightning Source LLC
Chambersburg PA
CBHW022040080426
42733CB00007B/918